AF488406

CURVED LINES IN TAMIL FOR TODDLERS

Dr.M. Dhanalakshmi M.A., M.Phil., B.Ed., SET., Ph.D.,

TAMIL UNLIMITED LLC
10 Maybelle Court, Mechanicsburg PA 17050.USA
tamilanitham.com

Title   *:Curved Lines in Tamil For Toddlers*

ISBN   *:979-8-9943628-3-9*

Subject   *:Juvenile nonfiction*

Language   *:Tamil,English*

Edition   *:Print 2026*

Book Size   *:8.000" x 8.000" (203mm x 203mm)*

Font   *:Tamil Virtual AcademyTAU Marutham,TAMUni-Tamil046*

Printing   *: IngramSpark*

Publication   *:TAMIL UNLIMITED LLC*
10 Maybelle Court, Mechanicsburg, PA,17050, USA.
+17178025889 ,+17177283999
tamilunltd@gmail.com

Pronunciation Guide

Vowels:

 There are five basic vowel sounds in Tamilஅ(/ă/), இ(/ĭ/), உ(/ŏŏ/), எ(/ĕ/), ஒ(/ŏ/). These sounds can be short and long. Short and long vowels have distinct forms to denote their pronunciation length. There are five short vowels and seven long vowels. When vowels take one second to pronounce, they are short vowels. A letter with one underline means it is a short sound. When vowels take two seconds to pronounce, they are long vowels. The letter with double underlines means it is a longer sound. Tamil vowels have two diphthongs. ஐ(/aɪ/) and ஔ (/aw/). அ(/ă/)and இ(/ĭ/) vowel sounds are within the ஐ(/aɪ/) syllable. அ(/ă/) and உ (/ŏŏ/) vowel sounds are with in the ஔ syllable. These two diphthongs are also long vowels.

Consonants:

There are eighteen consonants in Tamil. Tamil Consonants have a circle or a dot above them. Consonants take half a second to pronounce. The consonants are pronounced in three distinct ways, depending upon where the sound begins. Their pronunciation originates from the chest, throat,or nose.

The hard tone letters:

The hard sounding letters start from the chest with pressure. The thick lines indicate hardness.

க்   ச்   ட்   த்   ப்   ற்

The soft tone letters:

Soft-sounding letters are nasal sounds with minimal pressure and effort. The wavy lines indicate softness.

ங்   ஞ்   ண்   ந்   ம்   ன்

The mid tone letters:

Letters with in-between sounds initiate from the throat, which is between the chest and nose, so they are referred to as "in-between letters". The dotted lines indicate the mid sound characteristics.

ய்   ர்   ல்   வ்   ழ்   ள்

The Vowel_consonants:

When vowels are added to these consonants, they get their own form and sound. These letters are called vowel-consonant letters. Because of their association with vowels, the vowel-consonant letters also have either short or long pronunciation durations. The short pronunciations are indicated by an underline, and the long pronunciations are indicated by a double underline. The consonants and the vowel-consonants get their names based on where their initial sound begins.In this preliminary geometry for toddlers activity book, sight words are color-coded so the learner can recognize them without sounding out the letters. These color-coded words help children with accuracy, fluency, and speed in their reading, increasing comprehension and confidence.

அ
(/ă/),(/ŭ/),(/æ/),(/ʌ/)

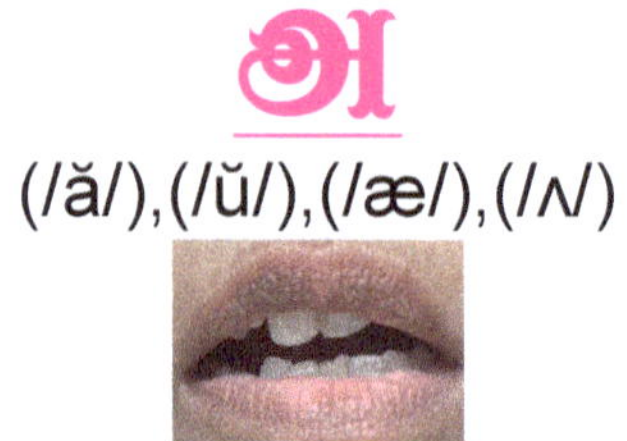

ஆ
(/ŏ/),(/ɒ/)

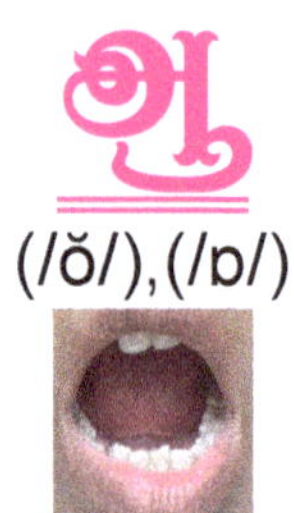

இ
(/ĭ/),(/ɪ/)

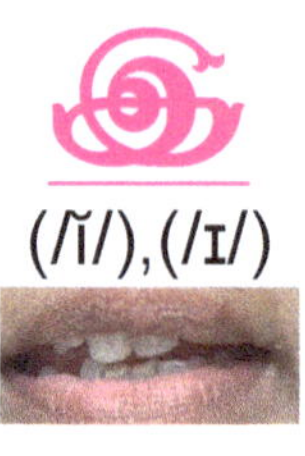

ஈ
(/ē/),(/i:/)

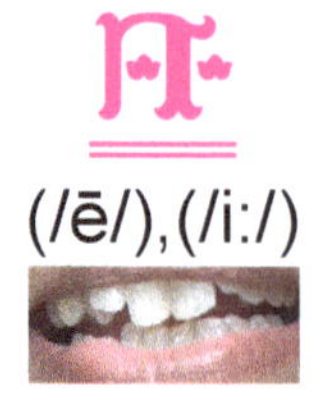

உ
(/ŏŏ/),(/ʊ/)

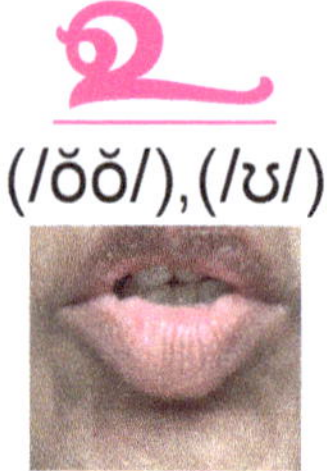

ஊ
(/u/),(/u:/)

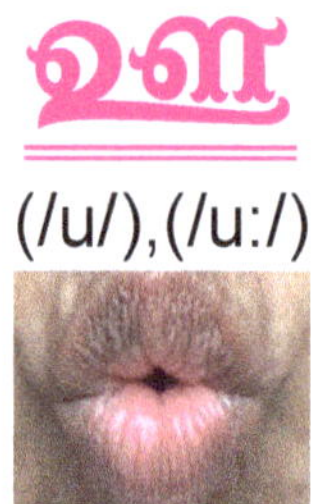

எ
(/ĕ/),(/e/)

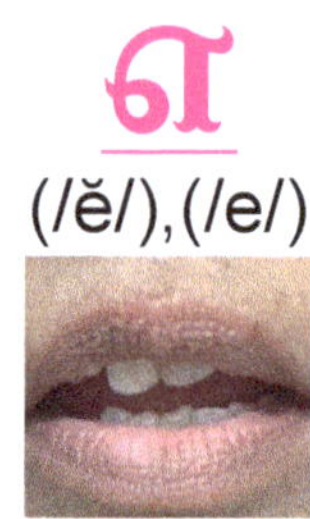

ஏ
(/ā/), (/eɪ/)

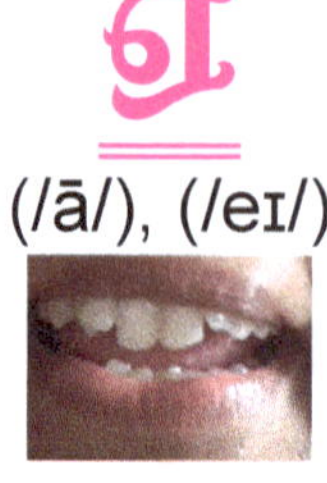

ஐ
/aɪ/

ஒ
(/ŏ/),(/ɔ:/)

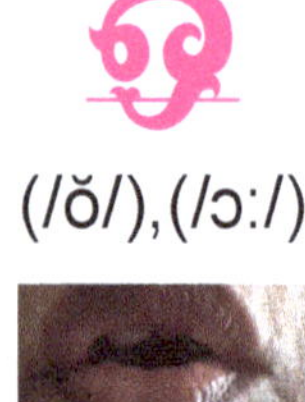

ஓ
(/ō/), (/ow/),(/oʊ/)

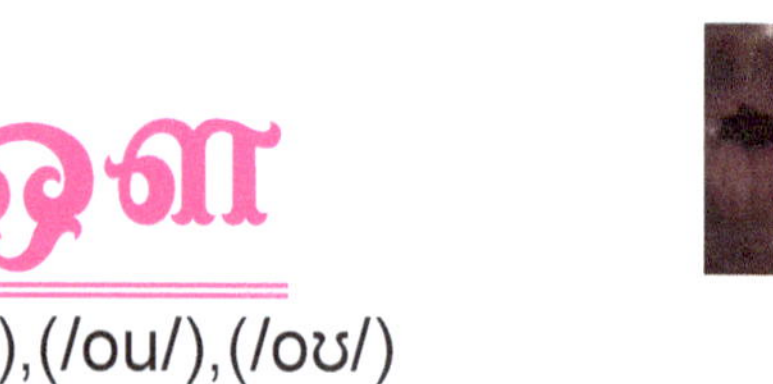
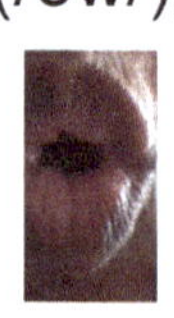

ஔ
(/aw/),(/ou/),(/oʊ/)

க்	ங்	ச்	ஞ்
/k/	/ŋ/	/tʃ/	/ɲ/
Say ik as in kite	Say ing as in song	Say ich as in march	Say inj as in banjo

ட்	ண்	த்	ந்
/t/	/n/	/t̪/	/n̪/
Say it as in time	Say in as in tan	Say ith as in thin	Say inth as in month

ப்	ம்	ய்	ர்
/p/	/m/	/j/	/r/
Say ip as in pan	Say im as in man	Say iy as in you	Say ir as in run

ல்	வ்	ழ்	ள்
/l/	/ʋ/	/ɻ/	/ɭ/
Say il as in level	Say iv as in van	Say izhl as in clung	Say ll as in black

ற்	ன்
/ɹ/,[r]	/n/
Say ir as in red	Say in as in fun

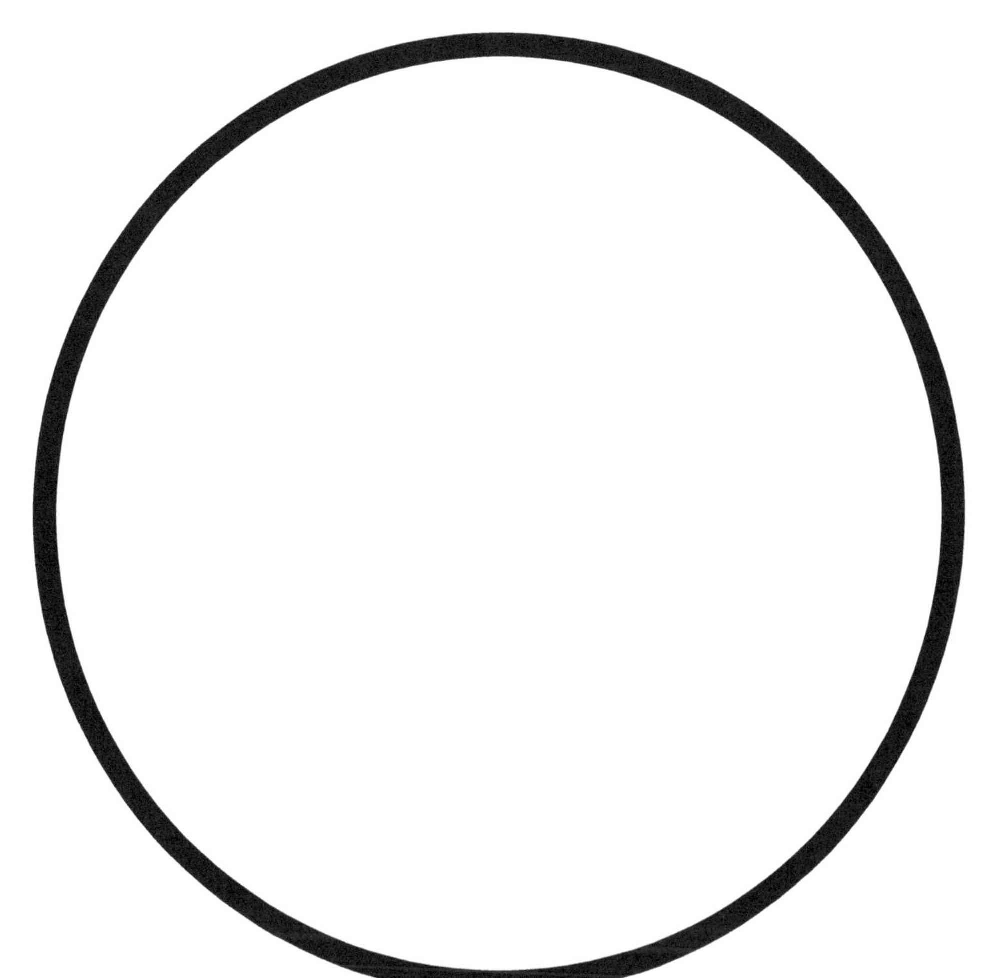

வட்டம், வட்டம், வட்டம்.
/vattam, vattam, vattam/
Circle, circle, circle.

வளையல் ஒரு வட்டம்.

/vaLLieyal ohru vattam/

Bangle is a circle.

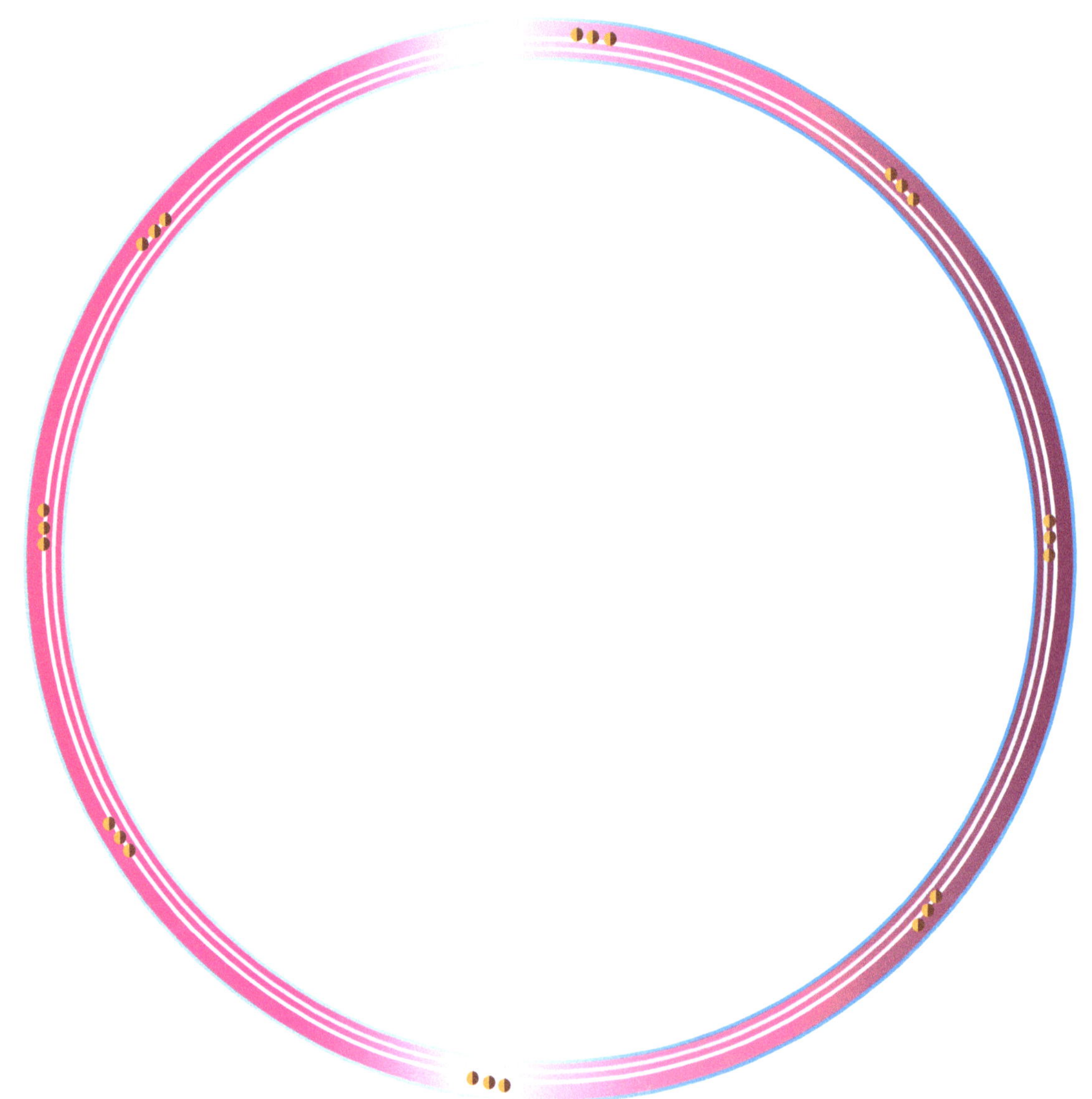

வட்டம், வட்டம், வட்டம்.

/vattam, vattam, vattam/

வட்டத்துக்குள் வட்டம் வடை.

/vattaththukkuLL vattam vadie/

Circle, circle, circle.
A circle with an inside circle is a wada.

வட்டம், வட்டம், வட்டம்.

/vattam, vattam, vattam/

வட்டத்தில் பாதி அரைவட்டம்.

/vattaththil pathi ahrievattam/

Circle, circle, circle.
Half of the circle is a semicircle.

அரைவட்டம், அரைவட்டம், அரைவட்டம்.

/ahrievattam, ahrievattam, ahrievattam/

வானவில் ஒரு அரைவட்டம்.

/vanavil ohru ahrievattam/

Semicircle, semicircle, semicircle.
A rainbow is a semicircle.

பிறை, பிறை, பிறை.

/pirrie, pirrie, pirrie/

வெட்டிக் கொள்ளும்

/vettik koLLLLum/

இரு வட்டங்கள்

/earu vattangaLL/

ஒரு பிறை.

/ohru pirrie/

Crescent, crescent, crescent.
Intersecting two circles is a crescent.

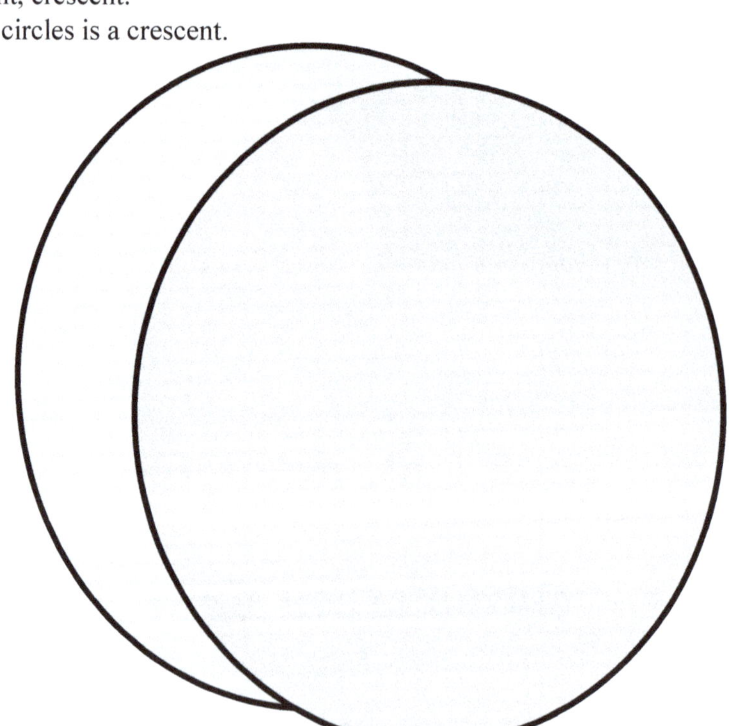

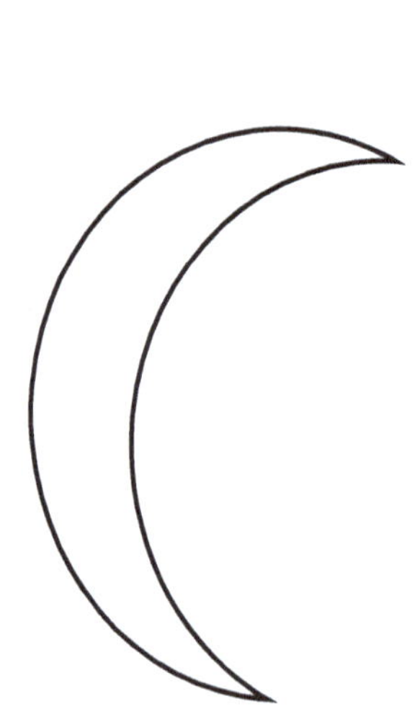

பிறை, பிறை, பிறை.

/pirrie, pirrie, pirrie/

வாழை ஒரு பிறை.

/vaahzhlie ohru pirrie/

Crescent, crescent, crescent.
Banana is a crescent.

வட்டம், வட்டம், வட்டம்.

/vattam, vattam, vattam/

நீளமாய் வளர்ந்த நீள்வட்டம்.

/neelamaaie vallarnththa neelvattam/

Circle, circle, circle.
Elongated, grown oval.

நீள்வட்டம், நீள்வட்டம், நீள்வட்டம்.

/neelvattam, neelvattam, neelvattam/

இக்கண்ணாடி ஒரு நீள்வட்டம்.

/eakkaNNNNadi ohru neelvattam/

Oval, oval, oval.
This mirror is an oval.

வட்டம், வட்டம், வட்டம்.

/vattam, vattam, vattam/

சுற்றிச் சுற்றி வரும் வட்டம் ஒரு சுருள்.

/sootRRi sootRRi varum vattam oru suruLL/

Circle, circle, circle.
A circle that goes around and around is a coil.

சுருள், சுருள், சுருள்.

/suruLL, suruLL, suruLL/

குச்சி மிட்டாய்க்குள்ளே ஒரு சுருள்.

/kuchchi mittaaikkuLLLay oru suruLL/

Coil, coil, coil.
Inside the lollipop is a coil.

Dictionary

அரை /**ahrie**/ (half)

இ /**eh**/ (this)

இரு /**iru**/ (two)

உள்ளே /**wullay**/ (inside)

ஒரு /**ohru**/ (one,a)

கண்ணாடி /**kaNNNNaadi**/ (mirror)

குச்சி /**Kutchchi**/ (stick)

குச்சிமிட்டாய் /**KutchchiMittaai**/ (lolipop)

கொள் /**kohLL**/ (have)

கொள்ளும் /*kohLLLLum*/ (it has)

சுருள் /**suruLL**/ (coil)

சுற்றி /**sootRRi**/ (around)

நீளமாய் /**neeLLamaaie**/ (elongate)

நீள்வட்டம் /**NeeLLVattam**/ (oval)

பிறை /**piRRie**/ (crescent)

மிட்டாய் /**Mittaai**/ (candy)

வடை /**vadie**/ (wada)

வட்டம் /**vattam**/ (circle)

வரும் /**varum**/ (will come)

வளர்ந்த /**vaLLarnththa**/ (grown)

வளையல் /**vaLLieyal**/ (bangle)

வானவில் /**vaanavil**/ (rainbow)

வாழை /**vaahzhlie**/ (banana)

வெட்டி /*vehtti*/ (That which cuts)

வெட்டு /*vehttu*/ (cut)